How exciting!

You're going on a great Adventure. For 50 days you'll stretch your spiritual muscles—in a way you may never have done before. If you stick with this Spiritual Adventure, you will:

▶ Find out that you have spiritual potential. You know some kids have potential in sports or music or art or science. But all kids have potential for God! All kids can learn to follow Jesus. You may have spiritual potential you're not even aware of. We hope this Adventure will help you start to discover it.

▶ Really get to know Jesus better. Every day you'll discover a special message from him in the Bible—meant for you.

▶ Find out why your church is really, really important. And hopefully, you'll learn to remember that Jesus truly is there every Sunday. You'll do that through a game— that will make it fun for you to search for him at Sunday school and church.

▶ Hook up to Jesus' power in tough situations. You'll feel good about yourself when you realize that Jesus can help you do what's right. Even adults on the Adventure will be working on this, because we all need to let Jesus show us how to improve. He knows we won't be perfect, but he wants to help us do better.

▶ Have a "mini-talk" with Jesus every day. We'll give you some ideas to get you started. But after 50 days, you'll be ready to do it on your own!

▶ Go on "seven secret missions" to do loving things for other people.

How's that for adventure?!!

HOW TO START THE 50-DAY ADVENTURE

When you go on an adventure, you usually come up against some challenges. They look hard at first. Sometimes they *are* hard. It will take you 50 days to meet all the challenges in this Spiritual Adventure. But remember: You'll only need to do a little bit each day.

Get ready—go! Make sure you check off all these boxes before the 50 days begin! Otherwise, you might start the Adventure lost.

☐ Read pages 3-12. They'll tell you about five "challenges" plus a bonus (an extra challenge) that you'll be doing in the coming 50 days.

☐ No points off for looking ahead! You might flip through the whole book to get an idea of what's coming. Each day is numbered. But the pages aren't complete yet. You'll be putting your own words, your own pictures, your favorite colors in this book. You'll be making it *your* special journal.

☐ Be careful—this is a little tricky! The Adventure really starts two days before Day 1. You'll want to be ready. Do the two warm-up days to give you a head start. They're on pages 13 and 14.

When the Adventure starts, try not to miss a day. But if you do, don't play catch-up. Just find the right day of the week and start over again there.

▶ If you get started and the Adventure seems too much for you, don't give up! If you *really* can't handle all five challenges, you'll still make progress if you stick with two or three. But you'll get the most out of the Adventure if you do all the steps.

▶ If you get stuck, remember that you can always ask for help. Talk to your mom or dad or another Christian adult.

CHALLENGE #1

Get Ready for Sunday on Saturday

Most kids get excited about famous athletes or singers or actors. In fact, if one of your personal heroes were going to be in church on Sunday, you might bring your sports cards for him to sign—or a tape or CD cover for her to autograph. You'd be pretty excited!

Did you know that Jesus was the big hero to many people in his time? Huge crowds followed him wherever he went. There was just something about him that was so special. People felt better when they were with him. The Bible has some wonderful stories about the strange things people did to get close to him—anything to be with Jesus!

When we go to Sunday school or church, Jesus is there to meet us. Sometimes we forget that. This challenge will help you remember how special it is to be with him on Sunday.

When you have heroes, you want to know everything about them—what kind of food they eat, how they spend their time, what they're *really* like. You want to get to know them better.

We can get to know Jesus better, and the better we know him, the more we'll love him.

These are ideas that will help you get ready to be with Jesus in Sunday school and church. Every Saturday, pick one thing to do. There's a box in front of each idea. Check the box when you've done the step it talks about. There are more ideas here than you'll need.

You don't have to choose all your ideas yet—the journal will tell you when to start.

▶ Ways to Get Ready for Sunday on Saturday

☐ Pick a song about Jesus that you like. As you get ready for Sunday, sing the song, hum it quietly, or crank it up on your stereo. Pay attention to the words. What do they tell you about Jesus?

☐ One Sunday morning, pretend that Jesus is physically with you. Put an extra chair for him at the breakfast table. Go for a short walk and talk with him. Let him sit in the car on the way to church.

☐ Draw a picture of Jesus with a whole lot of people around him. Draw yourself somewhere in the crowd, and write a couple of sentences about the strange things you would do to get closer to him. (In the Bible, one man got lowered through a hole his friends had dug in the roof!)

☐ Here are some words that describe Jesus: loving, holy, Lord, truthful, good, merciful. Look up a couple of them in the dictionary to find out more about what Jesus is like. Ask an adult about any definitions you don't understand.

☐ Pick one of your favorite stories about Jesus from the Bible. Get some friends to help you act it out. You could even

3

present this drama to your families. "Break a leg!" (That's drama talk for "Do a good job.") If you need ideas for a story to act out, look up Matthew 14:22-33 or Mark 10:46-52.

☐ Write a fill-in-the-blank love letter to Jesus. Use a separate sheet of paper.

Jesus, I'm glad I know you because _____. One thing I like about you is _____. When I think about meeting you in church on Sunday, I feel _____.

☐ Ask your parents some questions about their love for Jesus. (If your parents aren't Christians, pick another adult to talk to.) Here are some questions you could ask.

1. Why did you become a Christian?

2. What do you like best about Jesus?

3. Why do you go to our church?

4. What is one of the best things Jesus has done for you in your life?

5. How is your Adventure going?

☐ Write a poem to Jesus. You can use an **acrostic**. King David wrote acrostic poems to God. All you have to do is fill in each line with sentences or words that begin with the letter starting each line. Here's a sample using the word LOVE.

Now pick another word that tells something about Jesus, and write your own acrostic poem. You could use a word like GOOD, MERCY, LORD, or TRUE. **Have fun!**

Hard part! Show your acrostic poem to at least one other person.

☐ Spend time praying for your Sunday school teacher and pastor tomorrow. Ask Jesus to help you learn from them.

☐ Pretend you're inviting a friend who doesn't know Jesus to come to church with you. Write down some things you could say about Jesus to help your friend want to get to know him.

☐ Be original—come up with your own idea to get ready to meet Jesus on Sunday.

———————————◆———————————

Lord, I'm glad you love me!

Only you deserve my praise!

Very great is your love for me!

Every day I'll give you thanks!

#2 Discover a Special Message Every Day

Who is one of your heroes?

What if you got a special-delivery, personal letter from that hero? You'd probably read it over and over. You'd show it to your friends. You'd pay attention to the "secrets of success" your hero shared with you.

In this challenge, you'll be reading a special-delivery letter from the greatest hero of all—Jesus. He's worth getting to know. His "secrets of success" are better than anyone else's. He's a pro at showing you the best way to live.

The Bible is God's letter to us. Every day you'll read a little bit and discover a special message from Jesus—meant for you!

When everyone in your church is reading the Bible and listening to Jesus, wonderful things start to happen. People talk about loving Jesus. People want to show each other how much they love each other. People start doing special things for Jesus—things they were afraid to do before. People start saying things like, "I'm really glad I'm a Christian," or "I think our church is great."

This challenge will only take a few minutes each day. The journal will show you what to do.

▶ More Challenge!

On certain days in this journal, we'll ask you to memorize a short verse of the Bible. Why bother? Because in tough situations you need to remember what God has said, and your Bible isn't always around.

You'll probably be better at memorizing than your parents. Sometimes they'll be learning a longer section than you will. Encourage them to keep trying. Recite your verses to each other.

If you do well at memorizing these verses, you'll be a **mnemonic** expert (nih-MAHN-ik). Any special aid you use to help you memorize something is a mnemonic code. We'll give you some ideas in the journal.

SPECIAL DELIVERY

CHALLENGE #3

Hook Up to Jesus' Power

You don't know all the answers to the test and you want to copy your friend's paper....

It's your sister's turn to play the piano, but you want to keep on playing....

You feel stuffed, but that last piece of candy looks so good!...

Have you ever been in a situation like that, where it was hard to do the right thing?

Those tough spots are called temptations. When you're tempted, you want to do things you know Jesus wouldn't like. But when you welcome Jesus to your church and see how much he loves you, you want to please him.

Did you know there's something good about temptations? They give you the chance to practice doing what's right. Jesus is always there to help—you just need to hook up to his power. When you get in tough spots, you can ask Jesus for strength to say no to temptation.

That's what you'll be doing in this challenge. And the more you rely on Jesus to help you do what's right, the more confidence you'll have!

Look at the power-meter chart on the next page. Each day you'll ask Jesus to show you how you did at hooking up to his power in tough situations. Then you'll fill in a bar on the chart. By the end of the Adventure, you should be able to see how much better you've gotten at saying no to temptation—with Jesus' help!

▶ Hook-Up Alert!

Wouldn't it be nice if you got a warning signal every time a tough situation was about to come up? Many temptations will take you completely by surprise. But if you know where they're likely to hit, you can be ready.

Think of the places where you're often tempted.

☐ My room

☐ The playground

☐ My school

Add other places here.

_____

_____

_____

Now think of people or things that sometimes tempt you. Here are examples:

☐ My brother when he wants to play with my toys.

☐ My clothes when I don't want to put them away.

Now write your own here.

_____

_____

_____

These are areas where you'll need to be ready to plug into Jesus' power source. You'll need to be on Hook-Up Alert!

6

JESUS POWER METER

DOING WELL

COULD DO BETTER

Sample | SUN | MON | TUES | WED | THURS | FRI | SAT | SUN | MON | TUES | WED | THURS | FRI | SAT | SUN | MON | TUES | WED | THURS | FRI | SAT | SUN | MON | TUES | WED | THURS | FRI | SAT | SUN | MON | TUES | WED | THURS | FRI | SAT | SUN | MON | TUES | WED | THURS | FRI | SAT | SUN | MON | TUES | WED | THURS | FRI | SAT | SUN

1 2 3 4 5 6 7 8 9 10 11 12 13 14 15 16 17 18 19 20 21 22 23 24 25 26 27 28 29 30 31 32 33 34 35 36 37 38 39 40 41 42 43 44 45 46 47 48 49 50

Directions:
There are 50 bars here—one for each of the 50 days of this Adventure. Each day ask Jesus how you did at hooking up to his power. Then draw a squiggly "power line" in the bar. Draw the line all the way to the top if you hooked up to his power when you were tempted. Draw the line only partway to the top if you need to do better at hooking up to his power. The first bar is done as a sample.

▶ If you're not tempted by anything on a certain day, just leave that day's bar blank. You can pick up with the next day.

▶ At the end of 50 days you'll have a record of how well you did at hooking up to Jesus' power to do what's right.

▶ Remember: When you don't do as well as you could, Jesus is always ready to forgive you and to give you a fresh start.

#4 ~ Go on Seven Secret Missions

You'll enjoy this challenge. During the next 50 days, you'll do seven loving things for people who are not your best friends.

When Jesus was on earth he told his disciples many times, "My command is this: Love each other as I have loved you." He's still very good at loving people. When we welcome him to our church, we want to be loving just like he is.

It's easy to love people who are your best friends. That's not a hard challenge. This challenge is harder. You must do a loving thing for someone you don't normally show love to.

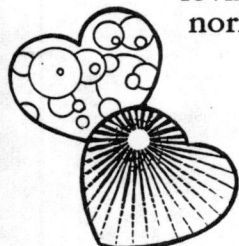

On the next page you'll write all of the seven secret missions you do in the next 50 days. You'll do one mission of love each week.

Now make this challenge even harder! Don't tell anyone about the loving things you do. Don't tell the person you're showing love to. Don't tell your best friend. Don't tell your Sunday school teacher. Don't even tell your parents. You can tell them you're going on a mission, but don't tell what loving act you do or the name of the person you do it for. After the 50-Day Adventure is over, you can show your parents page 9, but never tell anyone else.

Adults will be doing loving things for people, too. Watch them closely. See if you can tell what they're doing, but remember they can't tell you what they're doing. It's a secret for them, too.

IDEA: Try to do two of your missions of love for people who don't know Jesus.

Here are some possible missions. Maybe you could do one of them, but remember that the loving act is a secret.

■ You could thank an adult in your church for something special that person does in the worship service or Sunday school.

■ You could help a kid in your class with a difficult subject.

■ You could pick someone for your team who never gets picked until last.

■ You could make a happy-day card for someone who is sick or for an older person who lives alone.

What are some ideas you have?

_____

_____

_____

_____

Have fun with this challenge! Doing seven secret missions can make you feel just great.

My Seven Secret Missions

"Then your Father, who sees what is done in secret, will reward you"
(Matthew 6:4).

1. On _____ I secretly showed Christ's love to _____
   (DATE)   (NAME)
when I _____

2. On _____ I secretly showed Christ's love to _____
   (DATE)   (NAME)
when I _____

3. On _____ I secretly showed Christ's love to _____
   (DATE)   (NAME)
when I _____

4. On _____ I secretly showed Christ's love to _____
   (DATE)   (NAME)
when I _____

5. On _____ I secretly showed Christ's love to _____
   (DATE)   (NAME)
when I _____

6. On _____ I secretly showed Christ's love to _____
   (DATE)   (NAME)
when I _____

7. On _____ I secretly showed Christ's love to _____
   (DATE)   (NAME)
when I _____

#5 Do Mini-Talks with Jesus

When you're getting to know someone who's becoming a special friend, you spend time talking with each other about everything—things that make you happy, things that make you sad, your dreams, your fears, your secrets—just everything.

During this Adventure you'll be getting to know Jesus better. But talking to him isn't easy at first because you can't see him. Some people solve this problem by just rattling off the same words every night. That's no challenge! For the next 50 days, try using your own words when you talk to Jesus.

You don't have to pray for a long time. A couple of sentences would be great. But always remember that he's right there with you when you pray.

When something great has happened to you, tell him about it—he's happy for you. When a temptation is staring you in the face, ask Jesus for help. And don't forget to tell him what you like about him. That lets him know he's special to you.

To help you get going, you can use these sentence starters. Each day, finish a couple of these sentences in your own words.

▶ Sentence Starters

- Jesus, I think you're wonderful because...
- One way I'd like to be more like you is...
- This is the way I feel about the 50-Day Adventure today:...

- Please help me today to...
- I want to be more loving to...
- I know you were with me today because...
- I acted like you today when I...
- Please forgive me for not acting like you today when I...
- Thank you for doing these things for me today:...
- The special prayer I have for my church is...

IDEA: Try getting your mom or dad or another Christian adult to do mini-talks with Jesus, too. You could pray together and take turns completing the sentence starters.

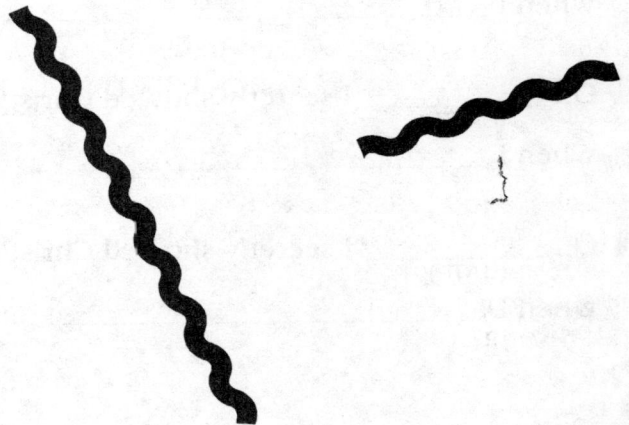

Bonus Challenge

Play the Sunday Search

This is a fun way to help you remember that Jesus is ready to meet you every Sunday. If you play this game, you could get a lot more excited about going to Sunday school and church.

Here are the rules for the Sunday Search.

RULE 1: Go to Sunday school or church every Sunday morning. Look for one way God speaks to you. He won't speak out loud. But he will let you know he's there and he's glad you came.

Here are some ways God speaks to people in church.

- Your teacher reads a Bible story and you hear a message in the verses for you.
- You sing a song and you think, *I'm really glad I love Jesus.*
- You do a fun page in your Sunday school book and learn how God wants you to live.
- Your pastor preaches and you know he's saying what God wants you to hear.

It's a funny thing. If you go to church expecting Jesus to speak to you, he will. And you'll know it!

RULE 2: Go to Sunday school or church every week and look for one way God uses you to speak to others. Obviously God speaks through the person who teaches Sunday school or sings in church. But God will also speak through you.

Here are some ways God might speak through you to other people in your church.

- You say good morning to someone who looks sad.

- You help a mother get her baby to stop crying.
- You set up chairs and clean your Sunday school area.
- You save a seat for a kid nobody likes.
- You say thank you to an usher.
- You hug your pastor and tell him how much you like him.

You see! God can speak through you to other people. In this Sunday Search, you'll discover seven ways he speaks through you on Sunday. You'll find one way each week.

RULE 3: Talk about rules 1 and 2. Share with your family or Christian friends how God speaks to you and through you each Sunday. Why not talk on the way home from church or during the noon meal?

On page 12 you'll find a chart. Use it to keep a record of how Christ speaks to you and through you.

You're going to be pleased with what you discover. You'll also have fun listening to what your parents or friends tell you about their Sunday Search.

START

The Sunday Search

SUNDAYS

1 How Christ spoke **TO** me: _____

How Christ spoke **THROUGH** me: _____

I TALKED ABOUT what happened with: _____

2 How Christ spoke **TO** me: _____

How Christ spoke **THROUGH** me: _____

I TALKED ABOUT what happened with: _____

3 How Christ spoke **TO** me: _____

How Christ spoke **THROUGH** me: _____

I TALKED ABOUT what happened with: _____

4 How Christ spoke **TO** me: _____

How Christ spoke **THROUGH** me: _____

I TALKED ABOUT what happened with: _____

5 How Christ spoke **TO** me: _____

How Christ spoke **THROUGH** me: _____

I TALKED ABOUT what happened with: _____

6 How Christ spoke **TO** me: _____

How Christ spoke **THROUGH** me: _____

I TALKED ABOUT what happened with: _____

7 How Christ spoke **TO** me: _____

How Christ spoke **THROUGH** me: _____

I TALKED ABOUT what happened with: _____

8 How Christ spoke **TO** me: _____

How Christ spoke **THROUGH** me: _____

I TALKED ABOUT what happened with: _____

Read
Psalm 145:17-21

▶ *The big Adventure starts in just two days. Today and tomorrow will warm you up and get you started.*

This is how King David paid God a compliment. It's a poem he set to music.

© LeFever/Weyna

Pretend you're writing your own chorus of praise to God. Use a favorite tune, such as "Jesus Loves Me." For the words of your song, pick small parts of Psalm 145:17-21. Write in this box the words you would pick to be in your song.

▶ *Read over the "Get Ready for Sunday on Saturday" ideas on pages 3 and 4. Which one do you think you'll do tomorrow?*

▶ *The big Adventure starts tomorrow.
Get a good night's sleep tonight!*

Read
Revelation 5:11-13

John is hearing all the angels in heaven singing about Jesus. Just as King David did, the angels are complimenting the Lord. In their song, Jesus is called "the Lamb."

What do you think this choir looked like? Draw your picture in the circle.

DOODLE SPACE

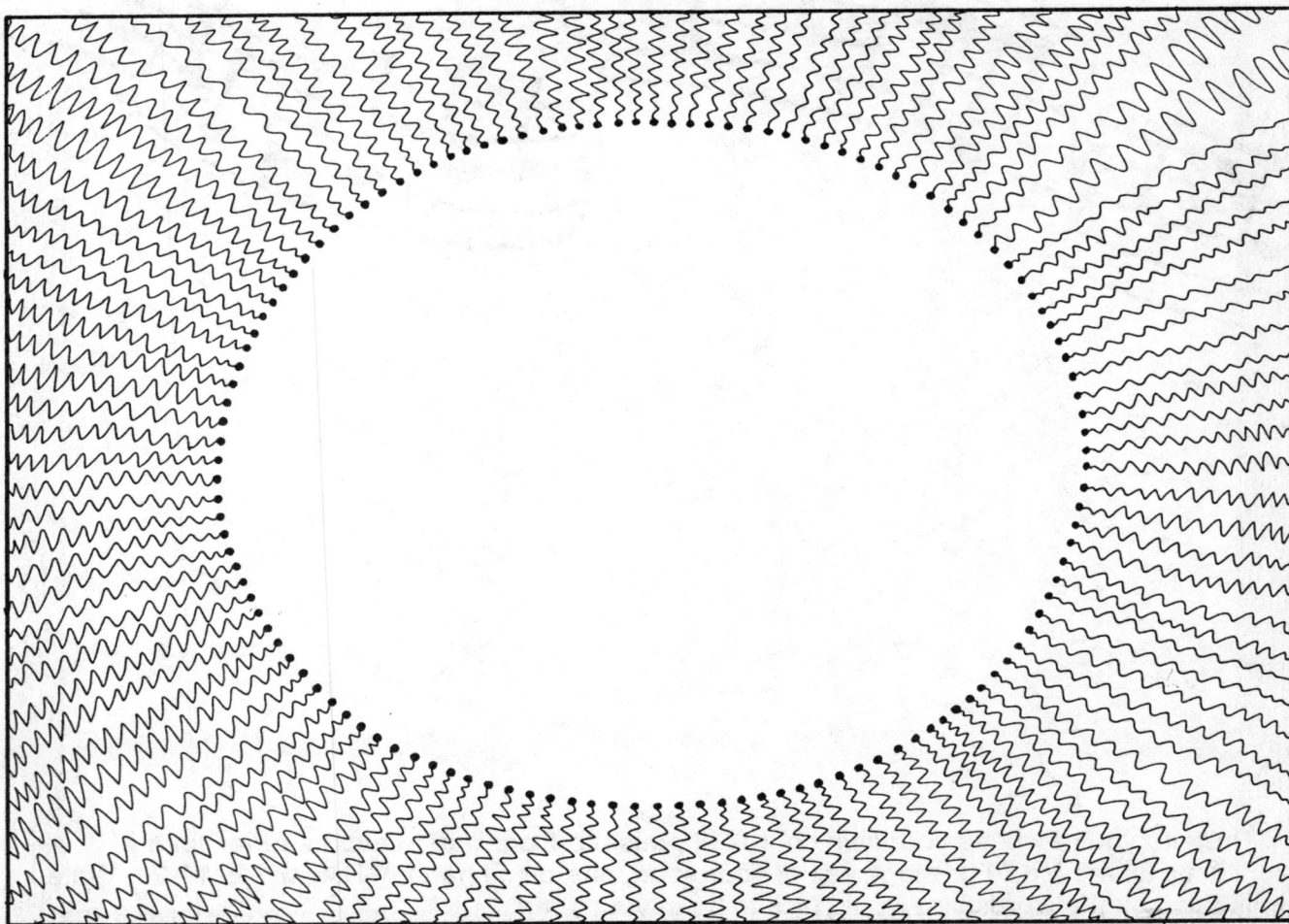

© LeFever/Weyna

▶ *Check off the "Get Ready for Sunday on Saturday" idea you did (pages 3 and 4).*

▶ *Don't forget—tomorrow you'll be going on the Sunday Search. Go back and read page 11 to review what to do.*

DAY 1 SUNDAY

Read
Revelation 5:11-13 again

We're told that the angels sang in a loud voice. Remember the Scripture song you made up on the Friday warm-up day? Sing it now—and loudly! You might want to get your mom or dad to sing it with you. How do you think Jesus feels when we sing praises to him?

CHURCH CHOIR

Draw a picture of your church choir singing praises to God. If you're in the children's choir, draw a red circle around yourself as you sing praises to God.

► *Are your Sunday Search results filled in on page 12?*

► *Have you had a mini-talk with Jesus today? (To review what to do, see page 10.)*

Read
Matthew 17:1-9

A lot of unusual things happened in this short story. Can you find three of them?

1._____
2._____
3._____

The disciples were scared when they saw Jesus and heard God the Father's voice. They fell facedown to the ground. If Jesus came to your church and you could see him, what do you think you would do?

Check as many as you think you would do.

___ I would jump up and down and clap.

___ I would fall facedown and worship him.

___ I wouldn't pay much attention.

___ I would start to sing praise songs to him.

___ I would run away in fear.

___ I would do what everyone else did.

___ I would try to get close and talk to him.

___ Here's something else I would do:

_____

In one sentence, write what Jesus wants us to learn from this story.

_____

_____

▶ *Did you have a mini-talk with Jesus today? (To review, look back on page 10.)*

▶ *Have you been filling in your Jesus power-meter chart on page 7?*

Read
2 Peter 1:16-18

▶ *Peter is talking about the story you read yesterday.*

Draw a stick-figure picture of the different parts of Peter's story.

If you don't know what the words **eyewitness** and **majesty** mean, look them up in the dictionary or ask an adult who is on the Adventure.

We were eyewitnesses of his majesty.	He received honor and glory from God.	God said, "This is my Son, whom I love."	God said, "With him I am well pleased."	We ourselves heard God's voice when we were with Jesus on the mountain.

If you have a hymnbook at home, look through it until you find a song that praises Jesus. (If you don't have a hymnbook, think of a song you sing in Sunday school or church.) Then sing that song to Jesus.

▶ *Have you decided what to do for your first secret mission? Go back and read page 8 to review that challenge.*

Read

1 Corinthians 10:13

▶ *Adults on the Adventure are reading this verse today, too.*

What temptations do you have? (Temptations are things you struggle with that make you want to do stuff Jesus wouldn't like.)

_____

_____

This verse tells you that Jesus won't let your temptations to do bad things become so strong that you have to give in to them. You're strong enough not to give in, if you rely on God's help. The middle part of this verse is printed here for you to memorize.

> God is faithful; he will not let you be tempted beyond what you can bear.

Adults are memorizing the whole verse. If your parents are on this Adventure, check up on them and see how well they're doing.

Here are three temptations. Read each one. Then write what you think Jesus would want you to do about it.

TEMPTATION

You find a wallet on the school playground and you're tempted to take $5 out of it before you hand it in.

TEMPTATION

Some of the kids call you a sissy because you won't try some "uppers" they got from the older kids.

TEMPTATION

Some of the kids start making fun of a mentally disabled kid in your class.

▶ *Have you been filling in your Jesus power-meter chart every day? If not, turn to page 7 and draw your power line for today.*

▶ *How are your mini-talks with Jesus going?*

THURSDAY

Review 1 Corinthians 10:13, and finish memorizing the part printed on page 18.

Write it six times on six different sheets of paper. Then stick the sheets of paper in places where you'll see the verse and remember that Jesus doesn't want us to give in to temptation. If we ask him, he'll help us do what is right, rather than what is wrong.

Stick your sheets of paper:

1. On a schoolbook for a subject you have trouble with. God can use the verse to remind you not to cheat.

2. On a mirror in your room. God can use it to remind you not to be mean to your parents or brothers and sisters.

3. On the TV top. God can use it to remind you that some TV programs aren't good for kids.

4. On the refrigerator. God can use it to remind you not to eat things that are bad for your body.

5. On your bike. God can use it to remind you to pick good friends.

Now come up with your own idea, and stick your last sheet of paper there.

Check on your parents (if they're doing the Adventure) and find out if they've memorized all of 1 Corinthians 10:13.

▶ *Are you still doing mini-talks with Jesus every day?*

▶ *Did you go on your first secret mission? Write what you did on page 9.*

Read
Deuteronomy 7:6

▶ *What a neat verse! You're a special person to God.*

Draw a picture of Jesus showing you how much he loves you. At the bottom of the picture, write: "I am special to Jesus. Jesus is special to me."

© LeFever/Weyna

_____

_____

_____

_____

_____

▶ *Review the "Get Ready for Sunday on Saturday" ideas on pages 3 and 4, and pick one to do tomorrow.*

▶ *Have you filled in your Jesus power-meter chart today?*

Read
John 15:9-17

Have you ever felt left out because nobody wanted to pick you for his or her team? That will never happen with God! He chose the disciples in Bible times, and he chooses us to be his friends, too.

Draw a face to show how you feel about each verse.

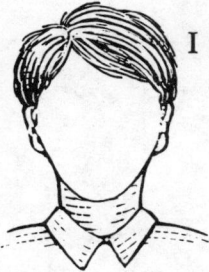

I [Jesus] have loved you.

You are my friends if you do what I command.

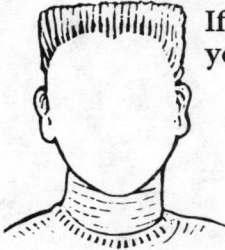

If you obey my commands, you will remain in my love.

I chose you.

Love each other as I have loved you.

This is my command: Love each other.

▶ *Today, do the thing you picked to "Get Ready for Sunday on Saturday." On pages 3 and 4, check off the idea you did.*

▶ *Don't forget—tomorrow you'll be going on the Sunday Search. (Read page 11 if you need to review the rules of the game.)*

Read
John 15:9-17 again

This Sunday you'll be with other Christians in Sunday school and church. You'll be praising God that he is love. Write an "I love you" note to Jesus. Tell him why you love him. Don't stop writing until you have at least 25 words. Or, make an "I love you" message for Jesus by talking into a tape recorder.

▶ *Did you do a mini-talk with Jesus today?*
▶ *Are your Sunday Search findings filled in on page 12?*

Read
Matthew 5:43-48

What does Jesus say about people who are nice only to the people who are nice to them?

_____

Think of one person who is hard for you to love. Ask Jesus to help you show love to that person. Then draw pictures in the squares of what might happen if you really could be loving toward this person. Each picture could show something different, or all your pictures could go together to make a story.

© LeFever/Weyna

How about doing your secret mission of love for the person you drew your pictures about? What is something you could do?

▶ *Don't forget to fill in your Jesus power-meter chart on page 7.*

▶ *Are you doing your mini-talks with Jesus?*

Read

1 Corinthians 13:1-13

Faith that is so strong it can move mountains

Giving all that I have to poor people

Being really smart and understanding all sorts of hard stuff

If I don't have love in my heart, what are those things worth?

_____

This is a very popular chapter of the Bible. Lots of people memorize it. What do you think: Do more people memorize it than actually live it?

_____

Yesterday you drew what might happen if you loved one person. Today draw a picture of one thing in our world that would be different if all Christians showed the kind of love the Bible is talking about. You may even want to put on a little drama about what would happen.

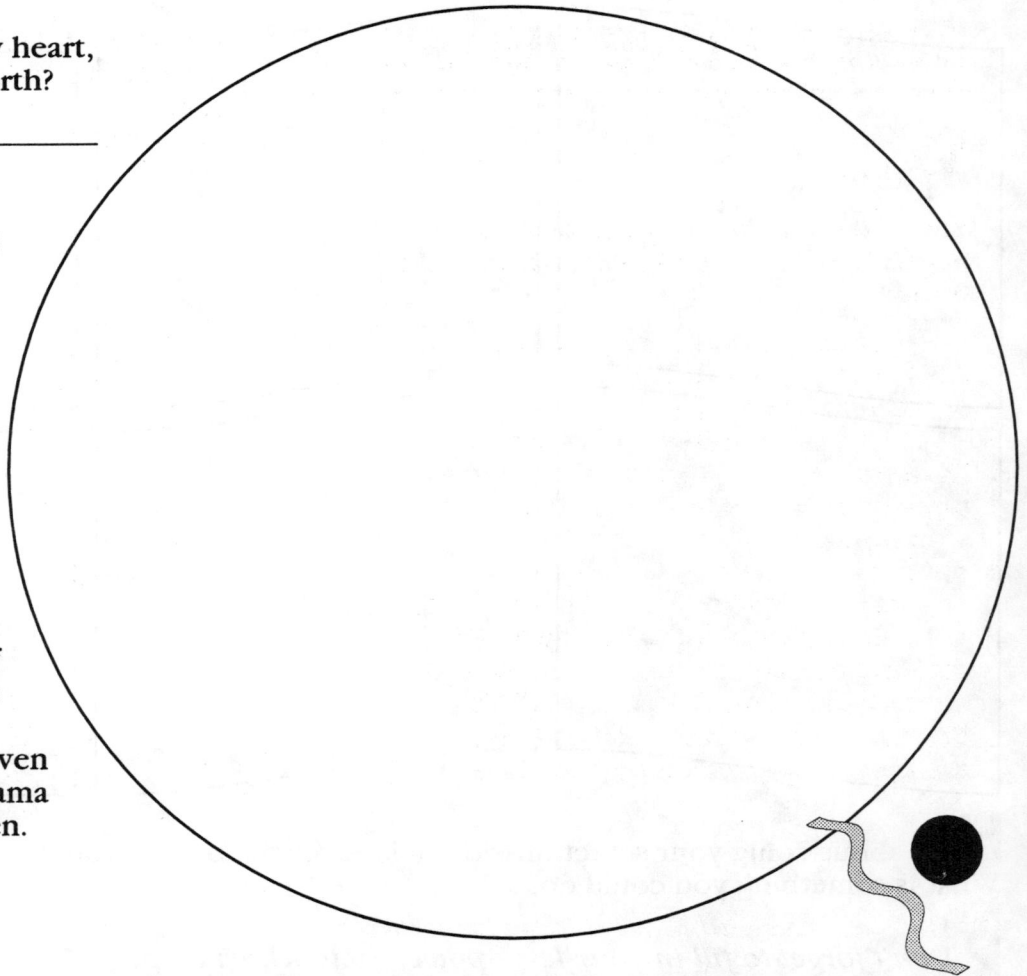

▶ *What will you do this week for your second secret mission of love?*

Read

1 Corinthians 13:1-13 again

▶ *Pick one verse out of the whole chapter that you would like to memorize.*

Write out your memory verse here.

_____

_____

Then sew the verse into construction paper to help you remember it.

SEW A LOVE VERSE

You'll need:

Your verse from 1 Corinthians 13, pencil, construction paper, needle, and thread.

After you have picked your verse, write it lightly in large letters on your construction paper.

Next, sketch designs to decorate your Love Verse. Use the ones shown here, or do original ones. Notice how the lines all start from a single spot and then branch out to form patterns.

Now sew your design—up, down, in, out until you have a finished design. Use different colored threads or put one design on top of another. Be creative! (If you don't like to sew, you could use colored toothpicks to make your design.)

Hang your design where you'll see it every day and be reminded of your Bible verse.

Why not make a Love Verse design for a friend?

From 62 Activities for Kids by Marlene LeFever © David C. Cook Publishing Co.

▶ *Did you do a mini-talk with Jesus today?*

▶ *Are you filling in your Jesus power-meter chart every day? Turn to page 7 and draw your power line for today.*

Read
Matthew 4:1-11

Every time Jesus says, "It is written," he is reciting an Old Testament Bible verse to the devil. How many times did Jesus quote from the Old Testament in these verses? _____

Circle the right answer. Jesus memorized Bible verses, so

1. I should, too.

2. I don't have to because it's hard work and he was so much smarter than I am.

Review the Bible verse you memorized yesterday. The next time you're tempted to do something unloving to another person, ask Jesus to bring that verse to your mind. What a great way to beat temptation!

If you haven't finished sewing your Love Verse, do that today. The instructions are on page 25.

"LOVE IS PATIENT, LOVE IS KIND..."

▶ *What did you do for your second secret mission? Write it down on page 9.*

▶ *Have you had a mini-talk with Jesus yet today?*

Read

Isaiah 6:3. Part of it is printed for you here.

> "Holy, holy, holy
> is the Lord Almighty;
> the whole earth
> is full of his glory."

Circle the words that tell what our Lord is like.

Put a star over words that could be names for Jesus.

Underline what you think is the most important word in this verse.

Put an exclamation point in front of each line that could be used as a song to sing praises to our Lord.

▶ *Look over the "Get Ready for Sunday on Saturday" ideas on pages 3 and 4. Pick one to do tomorrow.*

▶ *How's your Jesus power-meter? Are you pleased with the way your chart looks? Do you need to improve? If you haven't filled in your power line for today, turn to page 7 and do that now.*

Read
Mark 1:21-28

When the man with the evil spirit cried out, what name did he call Jesus?

"I know who you are— _____!"

Even the evil spirits call Christ **holy**. First write the dictionary definition of **holy** here.

_____

_____

_____

Now ask a Christian adult what **holy** means and write that person's definition here.

_____

_____

_____

_____

_____

THAT'S NOT WHAT "HOLY" MEANS!

Finally, write your own definition of **holy** in words that someone your age who is not a Christian could understand.

_____

_____

_____

▶ *Today's the day to do your "Get Ready for Sunday on Saturday" idea. Check it off on pages 3 and 4.*

▶ *Remember—tomorrow you'll be playing the Sunday Search when you go to Sunday school or church.*

Read
Mark 1:21-28 again

▶ *You'll be thinking today about the word **holy**.*

Do one or more of the following things to praise our holy God.

▶ **W**rite a Hebrew poem called an **acrostic**. Each line begins with the next letter in the word HOLY. In each line, praise Jesus for who he is. The first line is done for you. (If you want to see a sample of a finished acrostic, look at the LOVE poem on page 4.)

H *oly Jesus, I love you very much.*

O _____

L _____

Y _____

▶ Find several songs in the hymnbook that praise God for being holy. Or, see if you can find some songs about our holy God on your Christian music tapes.

▶ Write a 10-word sentence or paragraph explaining to a little kid what we mean when we say that we worship a holy God.

_____

_____

_____

_____

▶ *Did you fill in your Sunday Search results on page 12?*

▶ *What did you say to Jesus in your mini-talk today?*

Read
Ephesians 6:10-17

These verses show us how to be strong in the Lord—how to hook up to his power. To do that, we need to wear the armor of God.

Paul, the author of Ephesians, writes that the sword of the Spirit is the Word of God, the Bible. Are you getting to know the Bible? Are you sharpening your sword?

Write a "No Word" story. Make up a story about a kid who was in a tough situation and remembered what the Bible said to do. Draw story clues and tell what each clue means. Then share your "No Word" story with your mom or dad or your friends. Read this sample to see what a "No Word" story is like.

See if you can remember the two Bible verses you've learned so far. If not, go back and review them. They're on Day 4 and Day 11. Your sword's no good if it's dull and rusty. If your parents are on the Adventure, check with them and see how they're doing at memorizing their verses.

"NO WORD" STORY CLUES

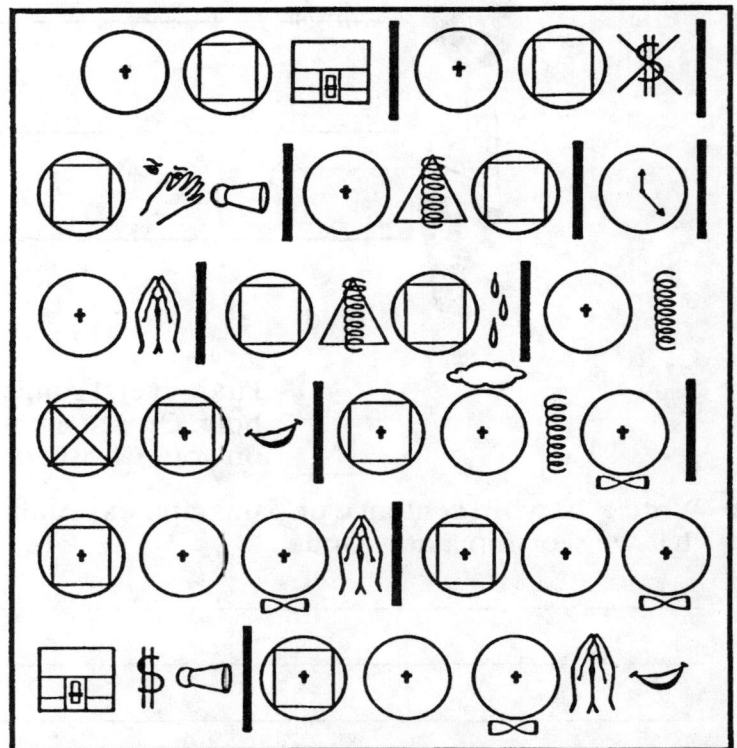

CHRISTIAN KID NON-CHRISTIAN KID CHRISTIAN KID'S FATHER TEARS PRAYER STORE

SCENE CHANGE STEALS MONEY BIKE HORN WORRY HAPPINESS NO

CONVERSATION PASSING TIME GOD

From 62 Activities for Kids by Marlene LeFever © David C. Cook Publishing Co.

▶ *Remember: Sharpening your sword of the Spirit helps you hook up to Jesus' power. How did you do today? Fill in your power-meter on page 7.*

DAY 17

TUESDAY

Read
1 John 2:3-6

Read these verses a second time, and put the message into one sentence.

_____

_____

Verse 6 says that if we are Christians, we must walk as Jesus did. In other words, we must do things that please God. Think back over the last few days. Make a list of three things you did that pleased God. (Maybe you hooked up to Jesus' power or did a secret mission of love. Those are things that please God.)

1. _____

2. _____

3. _____

Were there any things you did that were not pleasing to God?

_____

_____

Now circle the face that shows how you think Jesus feels about **all** of your actions this week.

Jesus loves you no matter what you do. When you know he loves you, you want to please him.

Write a prayer to Jesus, asking him to help you obey his words and act in ways that make him smile.

_____

_____

_____

_____

_____

▶ *One thing you can do that would please God is to go on a secret mission of love. What will be your mission this week?*

31

Read
1 John 2:3-6 again

▶ *Memorize verse 6:*
Whoever claims to live in him must walk as Jesus did.

One of the hardest places to live for Jesus is in our home. Think of six things you would be willing to do for Jesus in your home this week. Here are ideas. Use these or think of some of your own.

1. I promise to talk in a nice way to my folks all week.

2. I promise to go to bed when I'm told.

3. I promise not to tease or hurt my brothers or sisters.

4. I promise to do my chores all week without being told.

5. I promise to tell the truth.

6. I promise to do my best on my homework all week.

Add your own promises here.

_____

_____

_____

_____

PROMISE FLOWERS

Make promise flowers for each of your six promises and give the bouquet to your mom or dad. Next Wednesday talk together about how you kept your promises.

To make your flowers, fold a piece of construction paper in half. Draw each flower with one petal tip against the folded edge. Cut out the flower (double thickness) without cutting through the folded edge. Write a promise inside each flower. To make stems, tape a toothpick to one inside edge of each flower.

Make a bowl to put the flowers in. Mix 1 cup of flour, about 3 tablespoons of salt, and enough water to make a dough-like mixture. Roll it thin and cut it into strips. Grease a small oven-proof bowl and weave these strips together to form a basket. Pinch the ends of the strips together. Place a small roll of dough around the top of the container to form a finished edge. Bake at 250 degrees for four hours. Cool before removing the bowl. (Hint: Repair any cracks with white glue.)

Place a mound of clay in the bottom of your basket. Stick the toothpick flower stems into the clay and arrange your promise flowers in the basket.

It's fun to make promise flowers, but if you decide not to make them, you can still write your promises on sheets of paper and give them to your mom or dad.

▶ *How did your mini-talk with Jesus go today?*

▶ *Are you filling in your Jesus power-meter every day? Turn to page 7 and draw your power line for today.*

32

Read

1 John 2:3-6 again today

▶ *Review all the verses you've memorized so far, especially 1 John 2:6. The verses are printed on the inside back cover (Weeks 1-3).*

Jesus knows you want to please him most of the time. But all of us have times when we don't do what's right. What happens then? We need to ask for forgiveness. Spend some time thinking of areas in your life where you've pleased God lately. Then ask him to show you any areas where you've disappointed him and need to ask his forgiveness. These sentences may guide you.

Think about school. How have you pleased God at school? Do you need to ask his forgiveness for anything you've done at school lately to disappoint him?

Think about home. When lately have you lived the way you know Jesus would want you to? Are there ways you're not living the way you know a Christian kid should?

Think about the way you treat your brothers and sisters or your friends. Would Jesus be pleased?

IDEA: Use these sentence starters today when you talk to God:

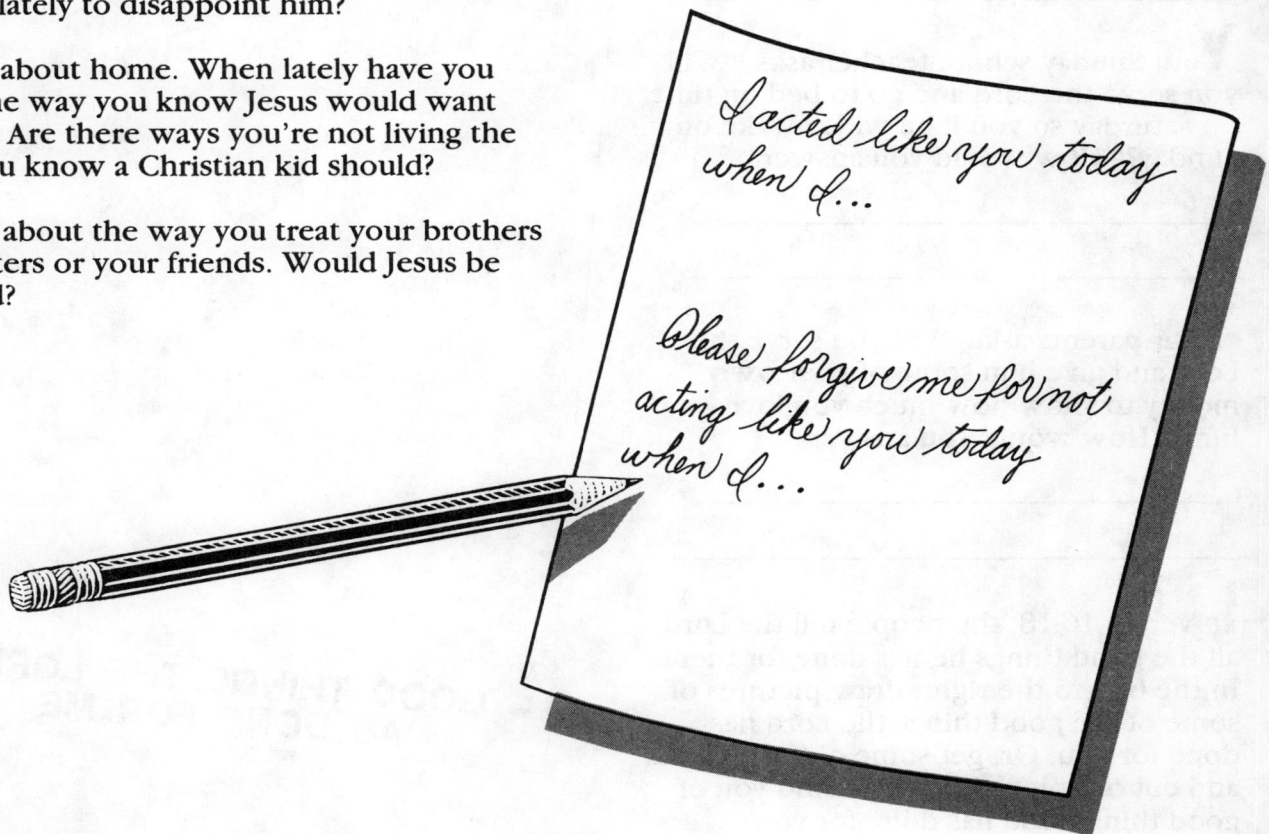

I acted like you today when I…

Please forgive me for not acting like you today when I…

▶ *If you've gone on a secret mission of love this week, Jesus is pleased about that. Write what you did on page 9.*

Read

Joshua 24:14-24

▶ *In this story the leader Joshua is talking to God's chosen people, the Israelites. He wants them to be very sure that they're going to serve the Lord.*

How many times does God make the Israelites say "We will serve the Lord"? _____ If your answer to the questions below is yes, write the same words the Israelites said, "We will serve the Lord."

Your pastor asks you, "Will you serve the Lord?" How would you answer?

_____

_____

Your Sunday school teacher asks, "Will you serve the Lord and go to bed on time on Saturday so you'll be wide awake on Sunday?" How would you answer?

_____

_____

Your parents ask, "Will you serve the Lord and give him some of your **own** money to show how much you love him?" How would you answer?

_____

_____

In verses 16-18, the people tell the Lord all the good things he has done for them. In the box to the right, draw pictures of some of the good things the Lord has done for you. Or, get some old magazines and cut out pictures that remind you of good things God has done for you.

GOOD THINGS THE LORD HAS DONE FOR ME

▶ *One way to serve the Lord is to hook up to his power. Have you filled in your power-meter?*

▶ *Look at the "Get Ready for Sunday on Saturday" ideas on pages 3 and 4. Pick something to do tomorrow. It will help you get excited about meeting Jesus in Sunday school or church.*

Memorize

Philippians 2:9-11

You have until Monday to do it. Paul, the author, is telling people that Jesus always put other people ahead of himself. He wasn't selfish. He never said, "Me first!" He was God and yet he was willing to be a servant for us because he loved us. In verses 9-11 we see how pleased God the Father was with the way his Son acted.

> **T**herefore God exalted him to the highest place and gave him the name that is above every name, that at the name of Jesus every knee should bow, in heaven and on earth and under the earth, and every tongue confess that Jesus Christ is Lord, to the glory of God the Father.

To help you memorize these verses of praise to Jesus:

1. Read them aloud several times—with lots of expression!

2. If there are any words you don't know or words that are used in new ways, ask a Christian adult to explain them to you.

3. Make up some hand motions to help you remember. For example, when you say "highest place," stand on your toes and point to the sky.

4. Write out the verses several times.

5. Practice the verses by singing them to a tune you know.

6. Say the verses for someone.

▶ *What did you do to "Get Ready for Sunday on Saturday"? Check off what you did on pages 3 and 4.*

▶ *Are you all set to play the Sunday Search tomorrow?*

Keep working on memorizing Philippians 2:9-11 (printed on page 35). This is a difficult job, but what wonderful praise verses! When you know them by heart you'll be able to say them to Jesus often. Praising him is like giving him a compliment. And when you pay someone a compliment, **you** usually feel better, too.

Think of some times when a person did a mean or unfair thing to someone else.

_____

_____

_____

Isn't it wonderful to know that Jesus *never* acts in mean or unfair ways? Use some special sentence starters to have a mini-talk with him:

DEAR JESUS, I'M GLAD YOU DON'T ACT LIKE _ _ _ _ _ _ _ _ _ _ _ _ _

_ _

_ _

I'M GLAD YOU DO ACT LIKE _ _ _ _ _ _ _

_ _

_ _

▶ *Have you written your Sunday Search findings on page 12?*

Read

Acts 9:36-42

▶ *Have you memorized Philippians 2:9-11? If so, repeat it aloud to Jesus. If you haven't finished, why not do it today? (The Scripture is printed on page 35.)*

Dorcas followed Jesus' example. She took a servant's job and worked for others, not herself. The Bible tells us she was always doing good and helping the poor. Jesus was so pleased with her behavior that her story is included in our Bible. What an honor!

Our church works best when people do things for each other and for God. Here are some jobs that people do for God and others in the church. Write the name of a person who does each job.

This person preaches:

_____

This person teaches:

_____

This person sings praises:

_____

This person cleans the church:

_____

This person makes new people feel glad they came:

_____

This person visits sick people:

_____

This person showed Christ's love to someone last week by going on a secret mission (if you did this, put your name here):

_____

▶ *How are you doing at hooking up to Jesus' power? Fill in your power line on page 7.*

▶ *Don't forget to do a mini-talk with Jesus!*

Read
2 Corinthians 9:1-5

▶ *In this story, Paul calls the Christians "saints."*

Can you put this story into a single sentence?

_____

_____

God loves it when we really do things for him—not just brag about doing things. Think back over the last few weeks. What are some things you have given to Jesus?

How have you given your time? Have you spent time talking to Jesus? Doing a loving thing for someone else? What have you done?

_____

_____

How have you given your money? Have you given your own money to help someone in need? To help your church?

_____

_____

How have you given your skills or your brainpower? Have you answered questions in Sunday school? Helped set up chairs? Passed out books? Sung songs? Read the Bible verse out loud to your class?

_____

_____

Which of these gifts is hardest for you to give? Why?

_____

_____

Do you think God is pleased with your giving? What would you like to do to improve?

_____

▶ *You can give your skills, your time, even some of your money to Jesus, by going on a secret mission of love. Think about what you'll do this week.*

Read
2 Corinthians 9:1-8

This is the same story you read yesterday, but there's a little more added to it. The new part is hard to understand. Read it several times and then write what it means in words so simple that someone two years younger than you could understand.

_____

_____

Did you do the Promise Flowers craft last Wednesday? If so, double check today to make sure you've kept all your promises. Those kept promises are gifts to God.

Sometimes the hardest thing for us to give is our money, especially money we've earned ourselves. Are you willing to give God some of your own money? If so, why not make a piggy bank to keep the money in? Every time you see the bank, it will remind you that the money in it is your gift to God.

You'll need a balloon; newspapers; runny, weak paste made of flour and water; straight pins; and paint.

Blow up the balloon and tie it with a string. Dip strips of newspaper in the runny paste, and slip them through two out-stretched fingers to remove extra paste. Cover the balloon with about four layers of newspaper strips. (Don't cover the spot where the top of the balloon has been tied. This will become the piggy's mouth.)

Wait until the paper has completely dried—at least 24 hours. Then cut the string and very slowly let the air out of the balloon. Remove the balloon.

Paint your piggy bank. Use straight pins to attach legs, eyes, ears, and a tail.

Put all the money you save for God into the mouth of your piggy. Empty your bank at the end of the Adventure and give the money to your church.

From 62 Activities for Kids by Marlene LeFever © David C. Cook Publishing Co.

▶ *The Adventure is half over today. What does your Jesus power-meter look like? Are you pleased with your progress? Do you need to improve?*

▶ *Have you had a mini-talk with Jesus today?*

Read
Matthew 26:69-75

Jesus had been arrested and was being tried. Peter must have been afraid that if he admitted he was Jesus' friend, he would be arrested, too. Maybe he would be killed. So he lied about knowing his best friend, Jesus. That's the normal thing to do. But it's not the Christlike thing (the thing Jesus would want you to do). Christians aren't "normal"! They do the hard thing.

Think of a time when you did the normal thing—but not the Christlike thing. Maybe you cheated so you would get a passing grade. Maybe you lied so you wouldn't get in big trouble. Maybe you laughed along with the other kids when they told trashy jokes.

What might have happened if you had done the Christlike thing? Write your answer by doing a stick figure story. In the first block, show what caused the problem. In the second block, show what you should have done. In the last block, show what might have happened if you had acted in a Christlike way.

▶ *Did you go on a secret mission of love this week? Write what you did on page 9.*

Read
Psalm 119:140

What are some of God's promises? One promise is written here. Can you think of two more? If you need help, go on to the next step. It will give you some ideas.

1. *God promises to be with us always.*

2. _____

3. _____

Pick an adult in your church who has been a Christian a long time. Ask that person these interview questions. Remember: You can do this interview over the phone.

The name of the adult I interviewed is

_____

INTERVIEW QUESTIONS

- What promises of God do you think are the most important for a kid my age to remember?
- What times can you think of when God's promises have held true for you?
- Based on everything you know about belonging to Jesus, what is the most important thing you would like to pass on to me?

▶ *Look over the "Get Ready for Sunday on Saturday" ideas on pages 3 and 4, and pick an idea to do tomorrow.*

▶ *Have you filled in your power-meter today on page 7?*

Read
John 16:5-7

▶ *Jesus is talking about sending the Holy Spirit to be with Christians and help them understand what's right and what's wrong.*

The Holy Spirit sometimes talks to you through your conscience. You just sense what's right. You know what will please Jesus and what will make him sad. Draw a picture of some of the good things the Holy Spirit can remind you to do.

© LeFever/Weyna

▶ *Today's the day to do your "Get Ready for Sunday on Saturday" idea. Check it off on pages 3 and 4.*

▶ *Remember: Tomorrow you'll be going on the Sunday Search!*

Read
John 16:5-7 again

Spend a couple of minutes thinking about your answer to this question before you even start to write anything: Someone asks you to explain who the Holy Spirit is. What do you say? (It might help you to read verses 8-15, too.) Write your answer in the box.

Now, show what you have written to an adult Christian. Ask that person what he or she would add. This is a hard question for adults, too!

▶ *Have you written your Sunday Search findings on page 12?*

▶ *What is something special you'd like to say to Jesus when you have your mini-talk?*

Read

1 Thessalonians 2:13

The Apostle Paul was thanking God because the church treated God's Word as very special. Sometimes Christians forget just how special God's Word is. But not spiritual adventurers! You've been looking for a special message from God in the Bible every day. What's one message you've discovered?

_____

_____

Can you think of some other things you've discovered? Write them on the notebook paper.

In the verse you read today, Paul says that God's Word was "at work" in the people who believed in Jesus. Unscramble the words to show how God's Word can be at work in you.

▶ Tells me how much God

elvos_____ me.

▶ Shows me what's **thrig** _____

and **grown** _____ .

▶ Helps me make good

icesoch_____ .

▶ Teaches me the **steb** _____

way to live.

Review all the verses from God's Word that you've learned so far. They're printed on the inside back cover (Weeks 1-4).

▶ *Finish this sentence starter when you do your mini-talk with Jesus today: I'm especially thankful for your Word because . . .*

▶ *Have you filled in your power-meter yet today?*

Read
James 1:22-25

In one sentence, write what James is saying in these four verses.

_____

_____

_____

Think of a Bible verse that you've obeyed. Write that verse here.

_____

_____

_____

OBEDIENT FOOT GAME

Play the Obedient Foot Game with your family or friends. To play the Obedient Foot Game, each player should draw and cut out ten of his own footprints from newspaper or construction paper.

Then each player should write ten obedience questions based on the Bible stories he or she knows. Many people in the Bible had to decide if they would obey or disobey God. We have to make the same decisions today. Will we obey the Bible and not cheat? Will we obey the Bible and honor our parents? Will we learn and follow the rules God has given because we know they're best for us?

Use the following samples to get started writing obedience questions. Each player should write ten questions.

SAMPLE QUESTIONS

Who did Jesus obey while he was on earth? Answer—God.

Who did Eve obey when she got into terrible trouble? Answer—Satan.

What man obeyed God and got a long sea journey out of it? Answer—Noah.

What father was willing to obey God even if it meant offering his own son as a sacrifice? Answer—Abraham.

What man obeyed God and brought frogs by the millions to Egypt? Answer—Moses.

Continue writing questions on the Bible stories you know. Pick someone who is not a player to read the questions.

RULES

1. Each player stands on one footprint and holds the other nine prints in his hand. Since he only has one print on the ground, he will have to stand on one foot. If he loses his balance at any point in the game, the player has to start over! (All players are standing at the same time.)

2. A reader gives the questions.

3. As soon as a player thinks he knows the answer he should place another footprint on the floor in front of him. The first player to put the print on the floor gets to answer the question.

4. If he answers the question correctly, the player stands on the next footprint. If he misses the question, he must pick up the footprint he just put on the floor. The next player to put his print on the floor gets to answer the question.

5. The first player to stand on his tenth footprint wins the Obedient Foot Game.

▶ *Think of a secret mission of love you'll do this week.*

Read
Hebrews 4:15, 16

▶ *In these verses Jesus is called our High Priest. These verses say Jesus was tempted just like we are.*

Check any of these sentences that are true.

___ Jesus was tempted to cheat.

___ Jesus was tempted not to share.

___ Jesus was tempted to lie.

___ Jesus was tempted to sass his mother and father.

___ Jesus was tempted to tell off a bully.

___ Jesus was tempted to steal.

___ Jesus was tempted not to pray and spend time worshiping God.

(If you checked every box, you're right.)

SASS? STEAL? CHEAT? LIE?

How does it make you feel to know that Jesus was tempted just like you are? He had some of the same feelings and some of the same hurts. Jesus didn't sin, but he understands your struggles.

These two verses are wonderful, but hard to memorize. Try it! If your parents are on this Adventure, they'll be memorizing them, too. Say them for each other.

> **T**his High Priest of ours understands our weaknesses, since he had the same temptations we do, though he never once gave way to them and sinned. So let us come boldly to the very throne of God and stay there to receive his mercy and to find grace to help us in our times of need (The Living Bible).

▶ *If you've hooked up to Jesus' power today, you've found what this memory verse is talking about—grace to help you in your time of need. Have you filled in your power-meter today?*

▶ *Don't forget your mini-talk with Jesus!*

Review
Hebrews 4:15, 16

Have you memorized it? Knowing what this Scripture means is more important than being able to say it word perfect. This Scripture means that when you're tempted, you can ask Jesus for help to do what's right. Show that you know what this means by writing an ending to this mini-story.

The teacher divides everyone into work groups. "Great! Just great!" Sarah sputters to herself as she looks around. "Not even one neat kid is in my group. Why do I always have to get stuck?"

Josh moves his chair around so Sarah can pull hers into the circle. "I'm glad you're here, Sarah. We need someone smart."

"Well, if you think I'm going to do all the work, you're crazy."

What might Josh be tempted to do or say?

_____

What if Josh did what Hebrews 4:15, 16 talks about? Write your answer by making up an ending to the story.

_____

_____

_____

_____

_____

When you've finished your ending, ask your mom or dad or another Christian adult to make up an ending to the story, too. Then compare your answers.

▶ *What secret mission of love did you go on this week? Write it down on page 9. You're getting lots of practice at being a "secret agent" for God!*

Read
Psalm 34:4-7

▶ *God is good. He hears the prayers of those in need.*

David wrote this psalm after the Lord had helped him out of a very difficult situation. Write or draw about a time when Jesus helped you out of a difficult situation or a time when you were afraid. Often he uses people to help us. Maybe you had a big project for school and God led you to an adult to help you figure out what to do. Or maybe you were afraid of a storm and God used your mom or dad to comfort you.

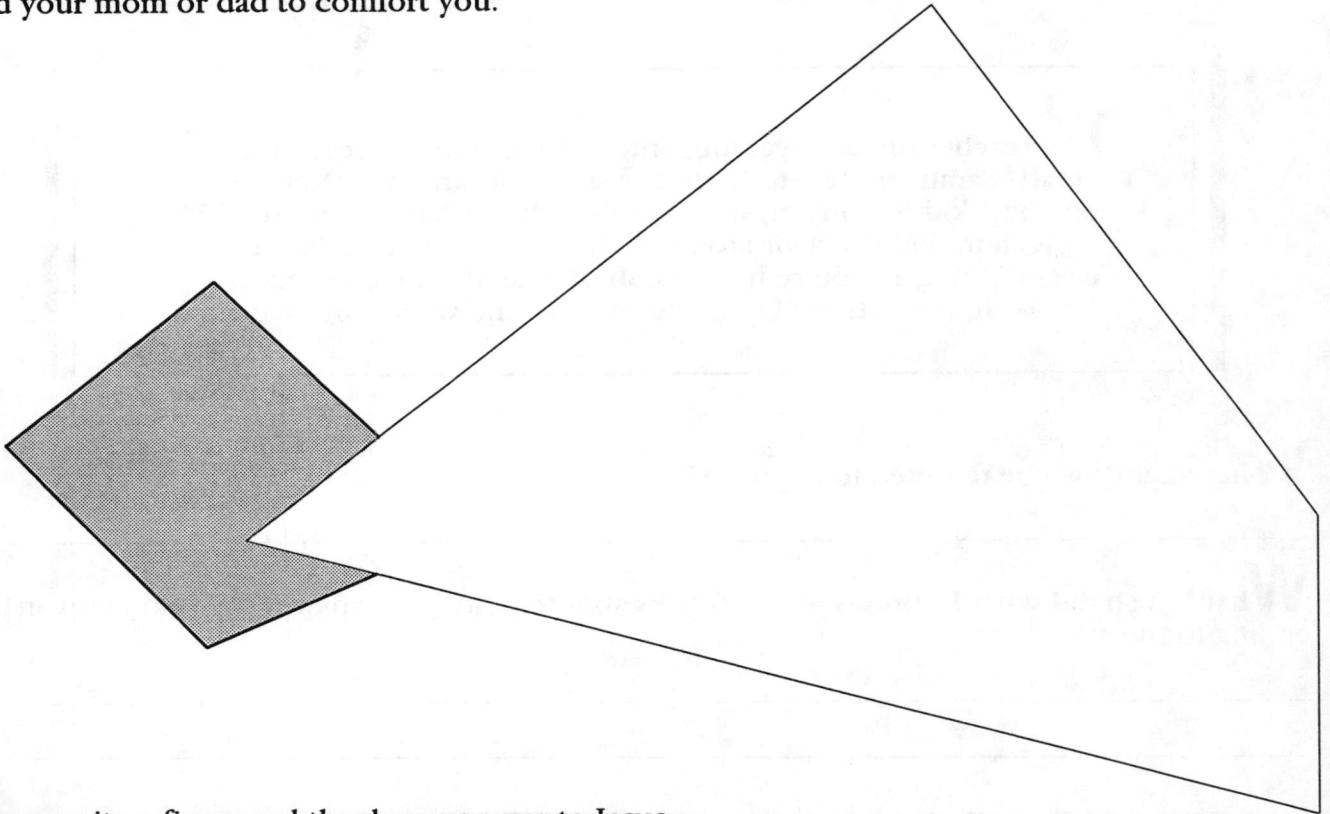

Now write a five word thank-you prayer to Jesus.

_____

_____

▶ *What "Get Ready for Sunday on Saturday" idea will you do tomorrow? Pick one from the list on pages 3 and 4.*

▶ *Are you pleased with your power-meter results? Is there anything you need to do to raise your power lines?*

Read
Matthew 7:7-12

Sometimes parents who love us don't give us everything we ask for. What are some reasons?

_____

_____

_____

God is your loving Heavenly Father. If he doesn't give you everything you ask for, it's because he knows what's best, just like your mom and dad. Sometimes we don't understand why God does what he does. But there are some things we can know for sure. Check any answers below that are right.

_____ God promises that everyone who is looking for a friendship with him can have it. All he or she has to do is ask.

_____ God wants to give us good things because he loves us.

_____ When God doesn't give us everything we ask for, we don't always understand and may even become angry. But by faith we know he loves us and wants what's best for us.

(If you checked all of them, you're right!)

Review all the Bible verses you've learned so far. They're printed on the inside back cover (Weeks 1-5).

▶ *Don't forget to do your "Get Ready for Sunday on Saturday" idea. Check it off on pages 3 and 4.*

▶ *Are you all set to go on the Sunday Search tomorrow?*

Read
Matthew 7:7-12 again

Read verse 12 slowly. Think of someone you've been unkind or selfish to. Write the person's name (or a code word) here, and ask your Heavenly Father to help you treat him or her the way you would want to be treated.

Draw a computer picture of a time when you treated someone who isn't a very good friend in a way that pleased Jesus.

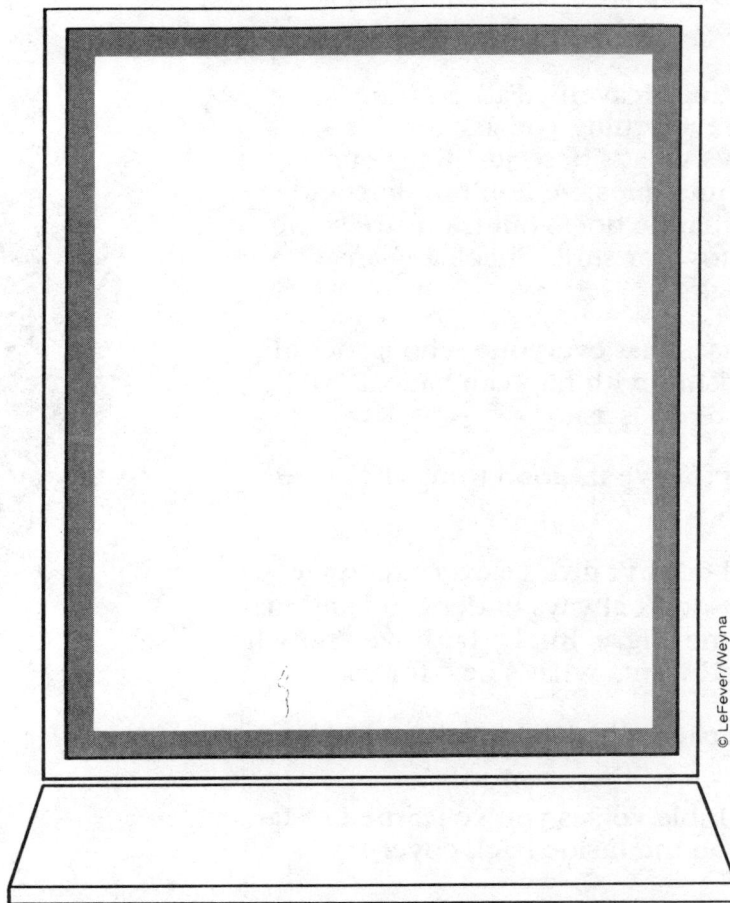

© LeFever/Weyna

▶ *What happened today when you played the Sunday Search? Write your answers on page 12.*

▶ *Have you done a mini-talk with Jesus today?*

Read
Matthew 6:5, 6

Hypocrites (HIP-oh-krits) say things they don't really mean. The hypocrites in this story didn't really mean what they were praying. They were just pretending so that they could impress people.

Jesus wants us to be honest and tell the truth when we pray. We can tell him whatever we're feeling. Think of something a kid might say to Jesus that he or she doesn't really mean. Then think of something the person could say instead that would be more honest. Read the example. Then fill in your own ideas on the blank lines.

EXAMPLE

Didn't Mean: You thank Jesus for a good day when it really wasn't a good day at all.

Honest Prayer: You thank Jesus for being with you even though you didn't have a good day.

Didn't Mean:

Honest Prayer:

▶ *Mini-talks with Jesus are a good way to pray what you really mean. Have you done a mini-talk with him today?*

▶ *How's your power-meter?*

▶ *This is a long but **great** story.*

Read
Acts 12:1-19

People were praying that Peter would get out of prison. God answered their prayers. How did they feel (check verse 16)?

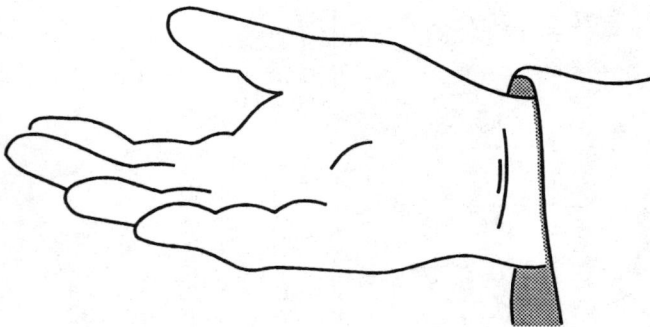

_____

© LeFever/Weyna

Think about some of the prayers God has answered for you. Then, above the first hand, draw a picture of a prayer that he answered in a way that surprised you.

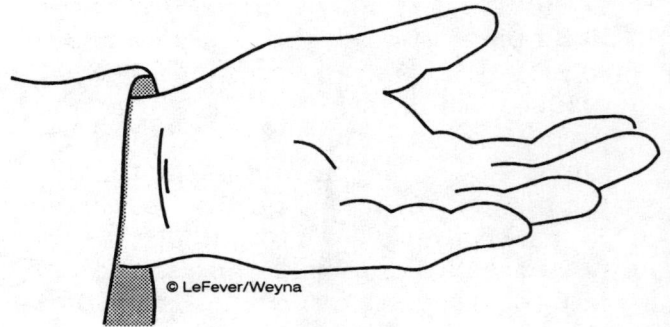

Above the second hand, draw a picture of something that you're still praying for. Pick something that's important to you. Don't forget to continue to pray. (Remember that God doesn't always answer the way we expect.)

▶ *You only have two more chances to go on a secret mission (during this Adventure, that is!). Think of something special to do this week.*

Review

the story in Acts 12:1-19

This is a great story about prayer. Think of something important that you can say about prayer in five words or less. If you get stuck, ask an adult to help. Write your five words here.

"WOODEN" PLAQUE

Make a "wooden" plaque out of your prayer words. Here's how. To make a plaque: Mix well and knead (press with your hands) 4 cups of flour, 1 cup of salt, and 1 1/2 cups of water for at least five minutes. If the mixture seems too dry, carefully add several more drops of water. You will get a ball of clay-like dough.

Roll out the dough and cut a shape like a piece of cut wood. Use a toothpick to press your prayer words into the plaque. Or roll small strips of dough and press them into your plaque to form raised words. Make a hole at the top of the plaque so you will be able to hang it.

Finish your plaque by adding decorations. For example, press a fork into the dough to make a design around the edges, put little balls of dough around the edges as a border, or cut out part of the dough along the edges to form a lacy design.

Bake your plaque in a 350-degree oven for about an hour. Remove it when it begins to have a light brown, wooden color. When it has cooled, shellac it, or paint it with clear fingernail polish. Put a colorful ribbon through the hole at the top of your plaque and hang it where you will see it often.

THOU ART MY GOD

TEACH MEE TO DO THY WILL

From 62 Activities for Kids by Marlene LeFever © David C. Cook Publishing Co.

► *Can you make your prayer words part of your mini-talk with Jesus today?*

► *Don't forget to fill in your power-meter chart!*

Read

and memorize the first part of Hebrews 12:2. It's printed here:

Let us fix our eyes on Jesus.

Fixing our eyes on Jesus doesn't mean carrying around a picture of him. It means living the way he wants us to live—hooking up to his power source.

What are two things you did in the last few days that showed your eyes were fixed on Jesus—that you tried to live the way he wanted you to? Write them down and draw a star in front of them.

1._____

_____

2._____

_____

Is there one thing you did last week that you would have done differently if your eyes had been fixed on Jesus?

_____

_____

▶ *If you've gone on a secret mission of love this week, you did something that showed your eyes were fixed on Jesus. Write what you did on page 9.*

Read
Hebrews 12:1

▶ *Here's a new part of the Scripture you read yesterday.*

This verse is about the many people of faith who want us to live for Jesus (that's what "running the race" means in this Scripture).

Circle the names of Christian people who want you to live for Jesus. Some of them may even be praying for you. Picture these people in the grandstands, cheering you on in the race.

NEIGHBOR   FATHER   SUNDAY SCHOOL TEACHERS   UNCLE   FRIENDS   CLUB LEADERS

GRANDFATHER   BABYSITTER   MOTHER

PASTOR   AUNT

BROTHER   SISTER

GRANDMOTHER

LIFE RACE REPORT CARD	
SUBJECT	GRADE
Speaking as Jesus wants me to	
Living at home as Jesus wants me to	
Acting the way Jesus wants me to at school	
Watching TV shows that Jesus wants me to watch	
Acting the way Jesus wants me to in Sunday school and church	
Acting toward parents the way Jesus wants me to	

Do you have any bad habits that you need to "throw off" to help you run a better race and live for Jesus?

_____

_____

Think of how you've run your life race this week. Then give yourself grades on your "Life Race Report Card."

▶ *Remember: A good habit is as hard to break as a bad habit. This is Day 41 of your Adventure. By now you're getting in the habit of hooking up to Jesus' power when you're tempted. Have you filled in your power-meter today?*

▶ *This is the next-to-the-last time you'll pick an idea to "Get Ready for Sunday on Saturday." What would you like to do tomorrow?*

Read
Titus 3:4, 5

Mark where you fall on the lines. For example, if you only cheat once in a while, you would put a mark near the center of the first line. The first one is a sample.

I never cheat |————————————✕————————————| I cheat often

Now mark where you fall.

I never cheat |————————————————————————| I cheat often

I obey parents |————————————————————————| I don't obey parents

I tell the truth |————————————————————————| I lie

I love everyone |————————————————————————| There are some people I choose not to love

Look at where you marked the lines. A chart like this makes us thankful that God saves us because he loves us, not because we've done good deeds. No one is good enough. But if we believe in Jesus as our Savior, he forgives us and washes away our sins.

Try these mini-talk sentence starters today. Use the ones that describe your thoughts.

▶ **Jesus, when I think about you as my Savior,**
   I feel . . .
   I'm thankful . . .
   I'm not sure . . .
   I believe . . .

▶ *Do another "Get Ready for Sunday on Saturday" idea from pages 3 and 4 and then check off what you did.*

▶ *Tomorrow you'll be going on your next-to-last Sunday Search (for this Adventure, at least)!*

Read

the verses from Titus 3 that are printed below. Then follow the "Mark Them Up" directions.

In the past we were foolish people, too. We did not obey, we were wrong, and we were slaves to many things our bodies wanted and enjoyed. We lived doing evil and being jealous. People hated us and we hated each other. But then the kindness and love of God our Savior was shown. He saved us because of his mercy, not because of good deeds we did to be right with God.... This teaching is true. And I want you to be sure that the people understand these things. Then those who believe in God will be careful to use their lives for doing good.

(Titus 3:3-5a, 8, the International Children's Bible)

Mark Them Up

▶ Underline all the things that are true of people who live their lives without Jesus. (Some of those things are true of Christians, too, but as we get to know Jesus better, he helps us to be more like him.)

▶ Someone says, "I can be good by myself. I don't need Jesus." Put two lines under the answer to show her she is wrong.

▶ Circle what people who love Jesus should spend their time doing.

Go back over the Bible verses you've learned so far. They're printed on the inside back cover (Weeks 1-6). If your parents are on the Adventure, check and see how their memory work is coming. Say your verses for each other.

▶ *Have you written your Sunday Search findings on page 12?*

Read

Acts 6:1-7

In the early church, widows had no way of making a living. So Christians gave them food. In this story some of the foreign widows were being missed. The church wanted to pick godly workers to make sure everyone had enough to eat.

Think of what you might be like when you grow up. Circle YES, NO, or MAYBE next to each answer.

ANSWERS

I want Jesus to help me:

YES	NO	MAYBE	Be a wise Christian adult who follows Jesus.
YES	NO	MAYBE	Care about what the Holy Spirit leads me to do, and try to do it.
YES	NO	MAYBE	Be willing to do even little jobs in the church.
YES	NO	MAYBE	Believe that what the Bible says is true.
YES	NO	MAYBE	Make sure people are treated fairly, as these men did.
YES	NO	MAYBE	Be like Stephen. (Careful. Remember that Stephen loved Jesus enough to die for him.)

Now circle any of the answers you think might end up being true.

Write a prayer to Jesus, telling him what kind of person you want to grow up to be.

_____

_____

_____

If you've been doing the challenges in this Adventure, you're forming habits that will help you grow up to be more like Jesus and his followers in the Bible.

▶ *One good habit is to do mini-talks with Jesus just about every day.*

▶ *How's your habit of hooking up to Jesus' power? Remember to fill in your power-meter today.*

Read
Acts 4:1-20

Peter and John were **witnesses** for Christ. That means they were telling people about Jesus. Someone asks you, "What were Peter and John like?" Think of three things you could say.

1. They were _____.
2. They were _____.
3. They were _____.

Circle any of those things that are also true of you.

One of the ways you could be a witness like Peter and John is to invite someone new to Sunday school or church or to a Christian club you go to. Maybe you could invite a kid in your neighborhood or a friend from school. Write the names of two people you might invite.

I could invite _____.

I could invite _____.

Pray for those people. Ask your mom or dad to pray with you and to help you find the right event to invite your friends to.

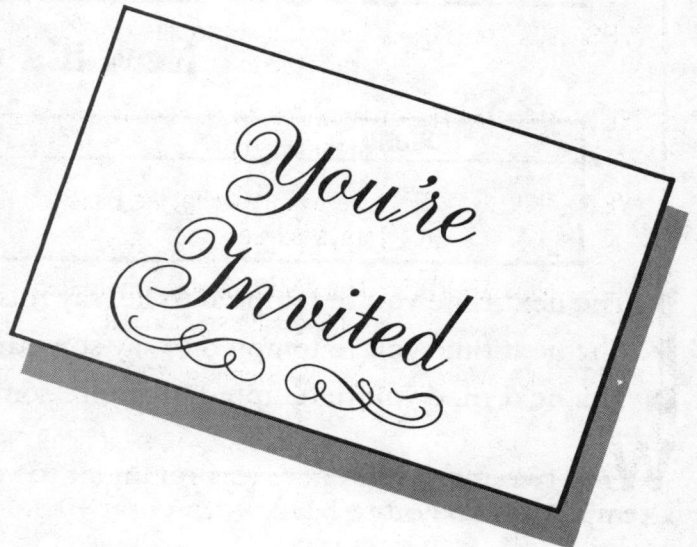

You're Invited

▶ *This week you'll go on your last secret mission of this Adventure. What's something special you could do?*

Read
Philippians 4:8

▶ *Paul gives us a list of very important things to think about.*

Memorize this verse. Adults on the Adventure will be learning it, too.

> . . . Whatever is true, whatever is noble, whatever is right, whatever is pure, whatever is lovely, whatever is admirable—if anything is excellent or praiseworthy—think about such things.

Make this verse more personal. Pick one word from the list in the verse. Then choose something to think about that fits the word.

Example

WORD	THINK ABOUT
True	What the Bible Says

Now it's your turn.

WORD	THINK ABOUT

▶ The next time you're tempted to lie, say this verse to yourself.

▶ The next time you're tempted to say something mean about someone, think about this verse.

▶ The next time you're tempted to ignore someone who needs a friend, think about this verse.

Write two more sentences as a reminder to yourself. For each sentence, fill in the blank with a temptation you often have.

The next time I'm tempted to_____, I'll say this verse to myself.

The next time I'm tempted to_____, I'll say this verse to myself.

▶ *If you say this verse to yourself when you're tempted, you're hooking up to Jesus' power. What does your power line look like today?*

▶ *Remember to do a mini-talk with Jesus!*

Follow some of the things that happened on Jesus' last full day of life. To help you, read Matthew 26:31-50.

Most people wouldn't have acted the way Jesus did. He treated people differently.

- How would most people have treated Peter?

_____

- How did Jesus treat Peter?

_____

- How would most people have treated the disciples when they fell asleep?

_____

- How did Jesus treat them?

_____

- How would most people have treated Judas?

_____

- How did Jesus treat him?

_____

- How do most people act around the kids in your class nobody likes?

_____

- How do you act around them?

_____

- How do most kids act around their folks?

_____

- How do you act around your folks?

_____

- How do most kids act around baby-sitters?

_____

- How do you act around them?

_____

- How do most kids act around teachers they don't enjoy?

_____

- How do you act around them?

_____

▶ *If you went on a secret mission of love this week, you acted the way Jesus would act. Write your mission on page 9.*

▶ *The authors of this book would like to get a personal letter from **you**! Tell us what you thought of this Adventure. On the inside back cover, you'll find our address and some ideas of what you might write.*

61

Read
Romans 5:6-8

Now read it again, and every time you see the word **we** or **us**, put in your name instead. Then write your name in the blanks in the box.

But God demonstrates his own

love for _____ in this: While
(YOUR NAME)

_____ was still a sinner,
(YOUR NAME)

Christ died for _____ .
(YOUR NAME)

ROMANS 5:8

This verse is written for ME

The Adventure is almost over. You've probably learned lots of things. What are a couple of them?

_____

_____

If you've kept up with the challenges in this Adventure, you've memorized seven Scriptures. They'll help you remember what God has said when you get in tough situations. Today would be a good day to review your verses. They're printed on the inside back cover.

▶ *Today you'll pick your last "Get Ready for Sunday on Saturday" idea on pages 3 and 4.*

▶ *Your Jesus power-meter is almost complete. You only have three more days to fill in. How do you feel about your progress?*

▶ *These sad verses tell about Jesus' death on the cross.*

Read
Luke 23:33-49

Even though Jesus had done nothing wrong, he took the punishment God would have given us for our sins. That was the most loving thing anyone could ever have done.

Write a poem telling Jesus how much you love him for dying for you. Use the word EASTER to write your poem. Each line should begin with the next letter in the word. The first two lines are done for you.

Everyone's sad that you had to die,

All of us say we almost could cry.

S _____

T _____

E _____

R _____

You might want to take your poem to church tomorrow to share with your Sunday school teacher.

▶ *Don't forget to check off your last "Get Ready for Sunday on Saturday" idea on pages 3 and 4.*

▶ *Tomorrow you'll play the Sunday Search for the last time during this Adventure!*

Read

John 20:1-18

▶ *No matter how well you know a story in the Bible, you can still learn new things when you read it.*

This is the familiar story of Jesus' resurrection.

Write Jesus a letter. These ideas will help you. When you have finished, read it aloud to Jesus.

Dear Jesus,

This is something I was reminded of when I read about your resurrection.

_____

_____

_____

_____

Two reasons I love you today are

1._____

_____

2._____

_____

Your friend for the rest of my life,

_____

▶ *Have you written your last Sunday Search findings on page 12?*

▶ *Fill in your last power line on your Jesus power-meter. How do you feel about your chart?*

▶ *Have you sent your personal letter to The Chapel of the Air? Our address and ideas for what you might write are on the inside back cover. Hope to hear from you!*